I0181969

The Playground Of Life

A Collection of Poems

Maria Elnora Savage

Copyright © 2022 by Maria Elnora Savage

The Playground of Life/Savage-1st ed.

Printed in the United States of America

All rights reserved.

No part of this book may be replicated or transmitted on any form or by any means, electronic or mechanical; including photocopying without permission in writing from the author.

ISBN: 978-1-953610-27-0

Cover Image by P.B. Red

1. Poems. 2. Poetry. 3. Verse. 4. Female Author. 5. Female Perspective.
4. Savage .

NFB Publishing/Amelia Press
<<<>>>
119 Dorchester Road
Buffalo, New York 14213
For more information please visit
nfbpublishing.com

This book is dedicated to my sister, Melanie who has always been there for me throughout our childhood side by side. She continues to be someone I can count on as I go though The Playground of Life!

Table of Contents

Section One

The Playground of Life

The Playground of Life

For many of us
Life simply begins and ends
On a playground…

At age two
You climb the slide
Beaming with pride
Reaching the top
Just to forget to sit
And tumble down

At age seven
You've mastered the slide
Moving on to the monkey bars
Holding on to the first rung
Trying hard to grab the next
Hitting the ground…

At age ten
The big kids come over
Tag you, so you join in
You may be small
Speed is on your side
You aren't "it" very long…you earned their respect

At age 13
You feel too cool for this old playground
Yet, here you are
Trying your first cigarette
Feeling cool, until you take that first drag
Coughing so much you know you'll never do that again

At age 17
You find yourself
Back at the playground
Playing basketball
Never had the height
But, speed is still on your side

Time moves on and you're 22
Sitting on the swings
Wondering which direction to choose
Staring up at the clear night sky
You close your eyes and pretend to fly

At 26
College has been conquered
You have a career
You're out on your own
It's time to propose
At the playground bench you get down on one knee

You're 30 now
Same old playground
Watching your two year old…

Climb the slide
Beaming with pride
Reaching the top
Just to forget to sit
And tumble down

Time moves on…

Here on this bench you sit
Watching your grandchildren play
At the playground
From slides to swings
Monkey bars to merry-go-rounds

What they do not know
Is that they are playing on
The Playground of Life….

Making friends for a day
Sometimes a lifetime
Sharing toys in a sandbox
Secrets under slides
Life spins in circles like a merry-go-round
Here at the playground of life!

Teeter Totter

You are always up
I am always down

I give
I care
While you sit up there

You're free
You're in the air
Why should you care?

Our teeter totter must be broken
I'm stuck here on the bottom

I'm the giver
You're the taker

My feet are always on the ground
Your head is in the air

I jump to try
To make you see
All that you're taking from me

Jumping higher
Giving you a chance
To balance us

Each time I jump
I fall even harder down
                         down
                                down
                                      to the cold hard ground.

Swings

I use to stand behind you
To give you the starting push
"Pump, pump!" I'd yell

You'd kick your feet wildly
Slowing, yourself down

I'd pull you back
And release you high
So high you felt like you were flying

Remembering when I use to wonder
"Will there ever be a time you'd fly on your own"

And then…
I stood behind you like I always did
Before I could give you that starting push
There you were…
flying on the swing all on your own!

So I started swinging beside you.
Now we could fly together
At times you were higher, other times I was
Swinging mostly in unison
Laughing freely as the wind hit our faces.

Knowing now
You'll always be able to fly on your own.

Merry-Go-Round

Around and around
Around again
We all go on
The merry-go-round

One child sits
On the inside
Holding on tight
Full of fright

One wild child
Sits on the edge
Leaning way back
Feeling the rush

One child's feet
Are on the ground
Holding the bars
And running around

On the merry-go-round
We all go around
Spinning in circles
Most never touching the ground

Bike

Letting go
"Don't let go," my child cries.
"I won't, " I simply reply.

Learning to ride a bike
One great challenge
Both for the parent and child

Even though I say I won't let go….
I know I must
I can not hold on to you; my child forever

I must let you go
"Don't let go," my child continues to cry.
"Just keep pedaling, eyes in front of you," I say.

Gaining speed, still lacking confidence
I let my child go.
Knowing I've done all I can

I've let go
When my child trusted me to hold on
Will this break our bond?

I've taught my child
Not to be afraid of the falls
To get back up again

Be prepared
Protected and
Follow the rules of the road

In the distance
I watch my child pedal, balance, steer
With eyes in front never looking back.

My child rides back to me
Eyes full of pride
Yelling " I did it, I did it!"

Me too! I think to myself
I let you go, all on your own.
Smiling, I say " let's go home!"

Climbing Trees

Climbing trees
Skinning knees
Walking branches like they're balance beams

Climbing trees
Feeling free
Swinging from branches like I'm on a trapeze

Climbing trees
Look at me
Hanging from branches just like a monkey

Climbing trees
Happy as can be
Sitting on branches just you and me

Climbing trees
Skinning knees
Knowing all these branches hold my memories

Beach

Waves are crashing
Children splashing
Couples kissing
Sand is sparkling

Watching my children
Digging for sand crabs
Collecting seashells
Building sand castles

Toes tucked in the sand
Water rushing over them
Smiling faces
Glistening eyes

Watching my children
Digging for treasure
Playing catch
Making moats

Hands covered with sand
Eating sandy sandwiches
Sitting at the waters edge
Until a crashing wave washes over

Watching my children
Soaked head to toe
Laughing
Running on the hot sand

Cool evening air
Settling in
Time to go
Walking on the hot sand

Reaching the boardwalk
We look back and see
Waves are still crashing
Children still splashing

Hill

Across the street
Through the old cemetery
Behind the church
Is the hill

Our Hill
Every day after school
We'd meet on the hill
To build our fort

On the hill
We'd dig for buried treasure
Finding rocks that glistened so bright
Pretending like we've found gold

We'd talk for hours
As we built our fort
Laughing and joking
No cares to be had

Playing 'til
The street lights shone
We knew then
It was time to head home

This was a time before
Video games and cell phones
A time of simple young innocence
A lost time

Across the street
I look out and see
The old cemetery
Surrounded by a fence

No longer a way to get
To our hill
Which has now
Become overgrown

Country Road

On this sunny day
I decided to come visit you
        So…
I drove down our old country road
Past the home where we grew up in

Slowed on down
To watch the kids playing in the yard

That used to be us …

Sittin' here lookin'
At the house that our family built

Over yonder is where
The chicken coop use to stand

In the front
There was the ol' horse corral

Nothing looks the same
Except for these trees

Down in those fields
We use to pick fruit til our fingers would bleed

Sitting here remembering
All our gatherings

I keep on going just
Past this hill

Here's where I find you
Under a family tree

So I pull off to the side
And lay my flowers down

Sit here next to you
Let the cool breeze hit my hair

Ain't' nothing like country air
Especially when it's just me and you

Neighborhood

Then…
When I was 8 I use to ride to the corner store
With a note from my mom
Return home with a pack cigarettes

Everyone knew my name
Walking in anywhere
There was no denying
My family

Cars pass by smile and wave
Neighbors come and snowplow the drive
We all would just
Help one another

Whether you needed a cup a sugar
Or milk to fill your baby's bottle
We were all there
Neighbors we cared

That was back when I felt a sense of
Community and humanity

Now…
My children and I
We take a bike ride
Cars fly by no one bothers
To even slow down

Take a walk around the town
No one smiles; Nor do they wave
Just act like we're invisible

Corner stores and penny candy
Have become extinct
Different cashier at these corner chain stores
No one knows my name… or my family

My car breaks down
Carrying children
Walking in 2 feet of snow
Cars keep just passing me by…
What happened to humanity?

SECTION TWO

THE ROLES WE HOLD

Holding Hands

Find your buddy
Find your partner
    and
Hold their hand
Hold on tight

Throughout my life
When I was younger
We always had a hand to hold

Crossing the street
Someone would always say
"Hold my hand, hold on tight"
And we'd cross it together
Hand in hand

Now that I'm grown
I find myself on my own

Reaching out to hold a hand
Finding out I'm all alone

I'm all alone on my own
No helping hand to hold

How am I going to do this on my own?
How am I going to face the world alone?

I'm on my own
I'm on my own

Without a partner
Without buddy
Without a hand to hold…

I'll cross the street
I'll find my way
I'll get through all life's twists and turns
All on my own
Without a hand to hold!

Best Friends

Jumping ropes
Skipping stones
Best friends

Casting lines
Down the shore
Sitting at the water's edge

Watching the waves
Truth or dare
Skinny dipping

Climbing trees
Being chased by bees
Best friends

Waterslides
Roller-coaster rides
Always fun with you by my side

Backyard barbeques
Public pools
Just trying to keep cool

Overalls to gowns
Make-up madness
Dress disasters

Crushes to lovers
Womanhood to motherhood
Best friends

Falling apart
And starting over
Best friends

Best friends
 Til the bittersweet
End!

Sisters

Sisters, more like polar opposites

Growing up we'd always fight
You kick me off the couch
Give me wedgies and grab the remote

You were the loud one
I was the quiet one

You were strong and capable
 I was always weak

You were beautiful
I was plain; so plain

No style or glamour to me

All the attention always on you
I became shy and subdued

You were popular
I was a nobody

But, still I was your sister

You took care of me
Defended me
Cooked for me
Walked with me
Truly cared for me

I never felt left behind…because you were always there
for me.
Sisters!

Tough

On the school bus
You'd try and trip me

Grab my backpack
Hold it hostage

In the classroom
You'd pick on me

Chase me around
The schoolyard

Constantly
You taunted me

You were tough
Until the crush

Around 8th grade
You changed

You'd save a seat for me
I sat with my friends instead

You offered to carry my books
I just kept on walking

In high school
You offered me a ride

I accepted
You let me drive

From tough to weak
From just one crush

This one crush
Exposed your vulnerability

I now hold the keys
Sitting in the driver's seat!

I guess your not that tough!

Underneath

Underneath the desk
You slipped me a note
To meet you

Underneath the tree
You said
You liked me

Underneath the slide
You held my hand
For the first time

Underneath the bleachers
You kissed my lips
To my surprise

Underneath my umbrella
I walked you home
And didn't want to let you go

Underneath the stars
I got down on one knee
And you agreed to be with me

Underneath the flowered arch
You said I do
And so did I

Underneath the covers
I see you
And all that's
Underneath!

Parenting

They call it parenting
So many books I've read
Stories I have listened to
Parenting
No one really prepares you for
Parenting
Up all night
Up all day
Endless diapers to be changed
Showers? What are those?
Don't you know I'm parenting!
Out of diapers
Cleaning floors
Baby proofing cabinet doors
Parenting
No, no, no
Is all I hear
Is all I say
Because I'm parenting
Out the door
On the bus
Back to showering!
Parenting
Parenting
Isn't this suppose to be fun?
Learning to read
To logarithms
School days are passing by
Back to no, no, NO!
You can't wear that
You can't be out that late
And who are you going to date?

Parenting
Parenting
College applications
Breakups and tears
Thinking the end may be near
Of all this parenting
Then the phone calls begin
The questions pour in
Parenting
Parenting, I say never ends!

Country At Heart

Heading into the city
Another family party
Girls in the backseat
Wearing matching dresses
Coordinating coats
Identical shoes
With their hair braided so perfectly.

At the party
The compliments pour in
Little ladies
So well mannered I hear
So sweet and
Proper with their curtsies

Little does anyone realize
They are country at heart
They'd rather be covered in mud
Running free
Then sitting here
Looking like dolls

Time to leave
As I close the car door
The hair ties are flying
Taking off their tights
They are country
Country at heart!

As we pull into our drive
They run out of the car
Feeling the wind in their hair
Mud between their toes
Country
Country at heart!

The can look and act the part
But, they'll always be
Country
Country at Heart!

Campfire

We all gather 'round
The campfire
Sitting in chairs
On logs
Or just standing near

Reminiscing
Stories retold
Embellished and exaggerated
Sharing laughs and jokes
And cold drinks

We all know
The painful truth
The diagnosis has come in
We look and see
You're growing thin

All secretly wishing
Clocks would stop
And the hours
Would not
Pass us by

We see you there
Sitting in your chair
Holding a beer
We all raise our hands
In a simple send off cheer

In this moment
The sky is clear
Stars illuminated everywhere
Campfire glowing
Sparks disappearing in the air

Suddenly, silence
Awkward silence
No one laughing
No jokes being told
Simple pure silence

Feeling your end is near
We see it clear
You show no fear
We shall try hard
Not to shed too many tears

Before you had a chance
To have wild days
And let your fire rage
The diagnosis had come in
And put your fire out.

'Round the campfire
We all gather
We set up your chair
With an ice cold beer
We bow our heads…wishing you could still be here

'Round the campfire

Fairy Tale

Life ain't no fairy tale
I grew up watching Cinderella
Still foolishly waiting
For my Prince Charming to come

I've seen more than I should have
Know more than I wanted
Because real life
Ain't no fairy tale

Been a witness to
The loss of life
Watched a man take a life
And another get life

In my days of roaming streets
Seen firsthand senseless shootings
And the corner dealings
Knew the thugs who were runnin' drugs

Life ain't no fairy tale
Pull back the curtain
You'll see all the hurtin'
I know that for certain

Living under bridges
Sleeping on park benches
Babies crying
Tempers flying

Trying hard to get it together
Working hard for all you have
Still not making ends meet
No money means no food

No fairy godmother to the rescue
Prince Charming is just a fairy tale
Going on working hard trying to making a living
And keep on living because

Life ain't no fairy tale!

All The Grounds Played On
and Roles We Hold

As children we grow up
Playing on different grounds

In my life I've played on
So many different playgrounds

From Backyards
To playgrounds
City streets
To county roads

From playing cards
Under street lights
To bike riding home
On pitch black streets

From swimming
 In public pools
To swamps and ponds
Full of mud

Swinging in trees
Climbing hills
Shooting guns
On country property

Running barefoot
Through the tall grass
On the hot sand and
Across the street

Catching fish
In lakes and streams
Ocean shores
To backyard canals

I am a daughter, sister, friend
I learned to listen and defend
Letting go of one role
To begin a new

From hustler to victim
Victor to loser

In the City
And the country
Rich and poor
We all have our roles

All the grounds I've played
And roles I hold
No one ever stopped to keep score
Pieces and players
Forever changing

At the creek chasing wood
Crossing down trees

Every day
A new adventure
Some of us playing
Others trying to survive

Fearless to fearful
Innocent to knowledgeable

All the grounds I've played
And roles I hold

I miss them all
From a time before

When I was fearless
Innocent and ignorant
A time of youthful bliss

www.ingramcontent.com/pod-product-compliance
Lightning Source LLC
Chambersburg PA
CBHW022348040426
42449CB00006B/775

* 9 7 8 1 9 5 3 6 1 0 2 7 0 *